Shapes & Letters

Reproducible Activity Sheets for Grades K-1

Troll Associates

Troll Teacher Time Savers provide a quick source of self-contained lessons and practice material, designed to be used as full-scale lessons or to make productive use of those precious extra minutes that sometimes turn up in the day's schedule.

Troll Teacher Time Savers can help you to prepare a made-to-order program for your students. Select the sequence of Time Savers that will meet your students' needs, and make as many photocopies of each page as you require. Since Time Savers include progressive levels of complexity and difficulty in each book, it is possible to individualize instruction, matching the needs of each student.

Those who need extra practice and reinforcement for catching up in their skills can benefit from Troll Teacher Time Savers, while other students can use Time Savers for enrichment or as a refresher for skills in which they haven't had recent practice. Time Savers can also be used to diagnose a student's knowledge and skills level, in order to see where extra practice is needed.

Time Savers can be used as homework assignments, classroom or small-group activities, shared learning with partners, or practice for standardized testing. See "Skills Index" to find the specific skill featured in each activity.

SKILLS INDEX

 # Color the Shapes

Color the big and little
shapes that look like me!!

Color the Shapes

Color the big
and little shapes
that look like me!

Name_____ **Date** _____

4

 # Shapes & Things

Color the things
that look like me!

Name_____ Date _____

5

Shapes & Things

Color the things that look like me!

Name_____ **Date**_____

Shapes & Things

Color the things that look like me!

Name _____   Date _____

7

Shapes & Things

Color the things
that look like me!

Name_____ **Date**_____

8

Copy This!

Copy the patterns.

What's Missing?

**What's missing?
Finish the animals.**

Name_____ **Date** _____

10

Family Fun

Find the baby!
Draw a line to
the right baby.

cat

cub

bear

chick

horse

kitten

chicken

colt

Name _____

Date _____

Small Shapes

Circle the **smaller** object in each box.

Name_____ Date_____

Big Shapes

  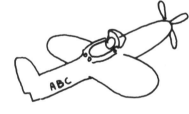 

Circle the object that is **bigger** in each box.

Name _____ **Date** _____

13

Match the Shapes

Cut out the foods and attach them on the correct shapes in the refrigerator.

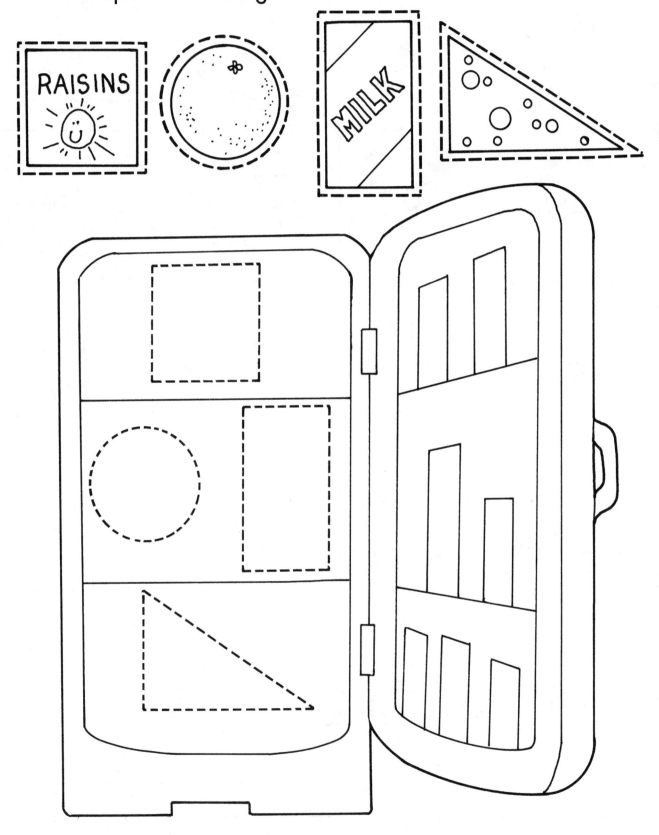

RAISINS

MILK

Color the Circles

In each row find two things that have the same shape.
Color them red.

Name_____ **Date**_____

15

Color the Rectangles

In each row find two things that have the same shape.
Color them green.

 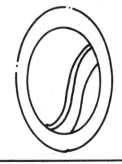  

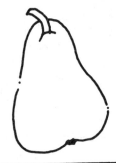  

Name _____   Date _____

16

Color the Squares

In each row find two things that have the same shape.
Color them blue.

Name _____

Date _____

17

Color the Triangles

In each row find two things that have the same shape.
Color them orange.

Name_____ **Date** _____

18

Find the Circles

Use your red crayon. Color all the circles (O).

Name_____ **Date** _____

19

Find the Squares

Use your green crayon. Color all the squares (□).

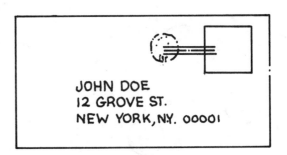

JOHN DOE
12 GROVE ST.
NEW YORK, NY. 00001

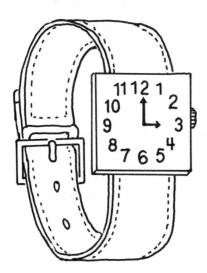

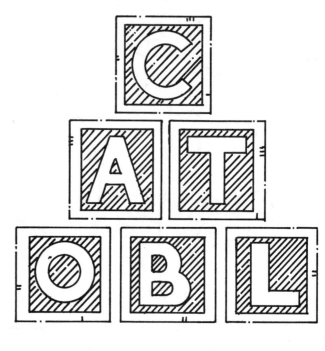

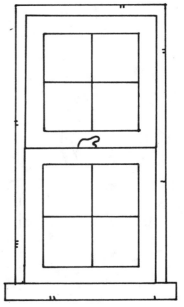

Name_____ **Date**_____

20

Find the Rectangles

Use your yellow crayon. Color all the rectangles (▯▭).

Name_____ Date_____

Find the Triangles

Use your blue crayon. Color all the triangles (△◁).

Name_____ Date_____

Find the Pattern

Draw the thing that will finish the pattern in each row.

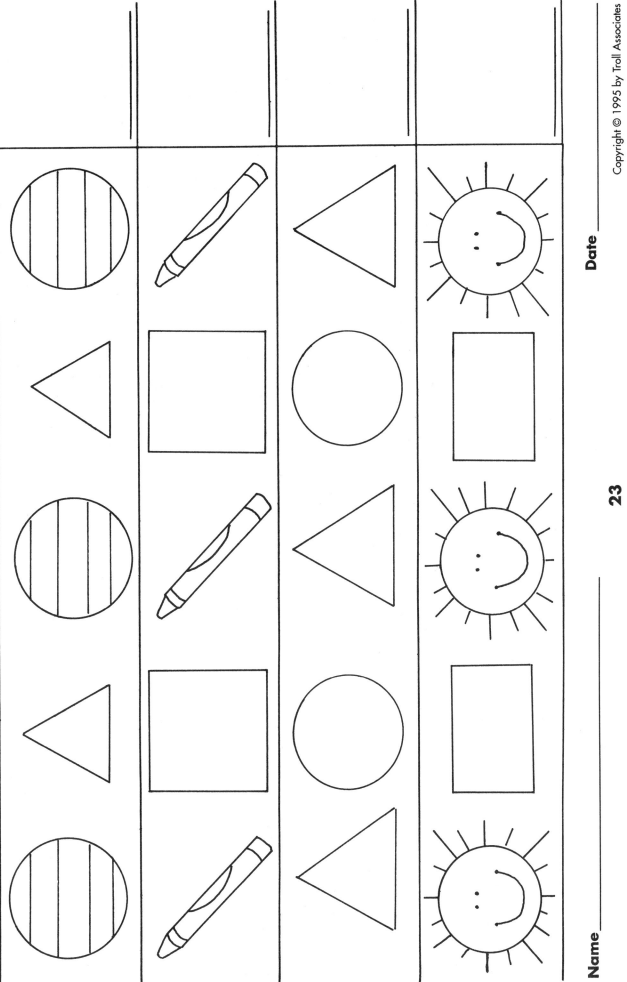

Date

23

Name

Finish the Pattern

Draw the thing that will finish the pattern in each row.

Name _____

Date _____

24

Follow the Pattern

Draw the things that will finish the pattern in each row.

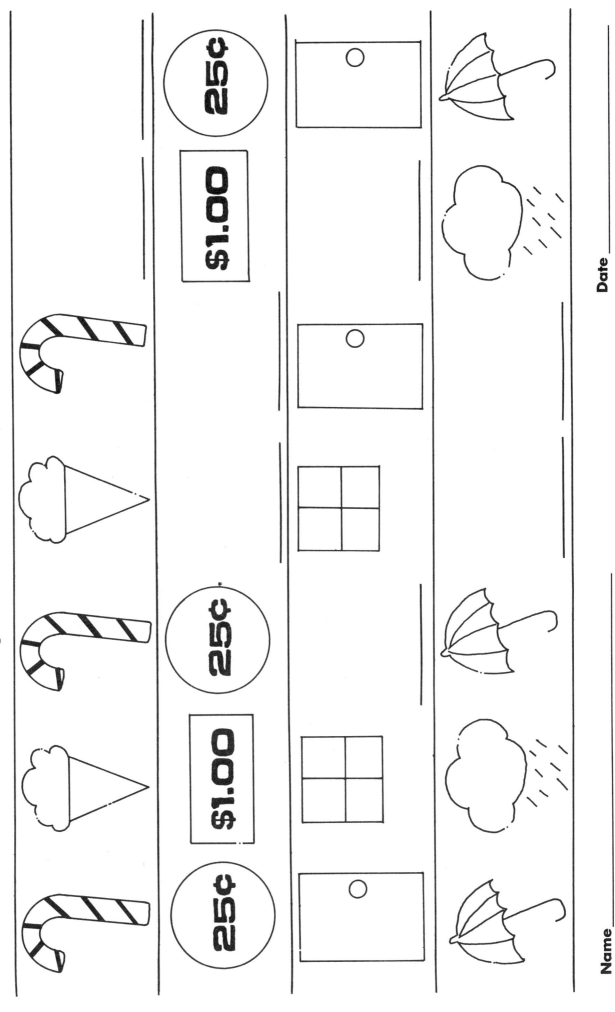

Name _____

Date _____

25

Cut & Paste

Cut out the parts of the bus and attach them in the correct shapes on the bus.

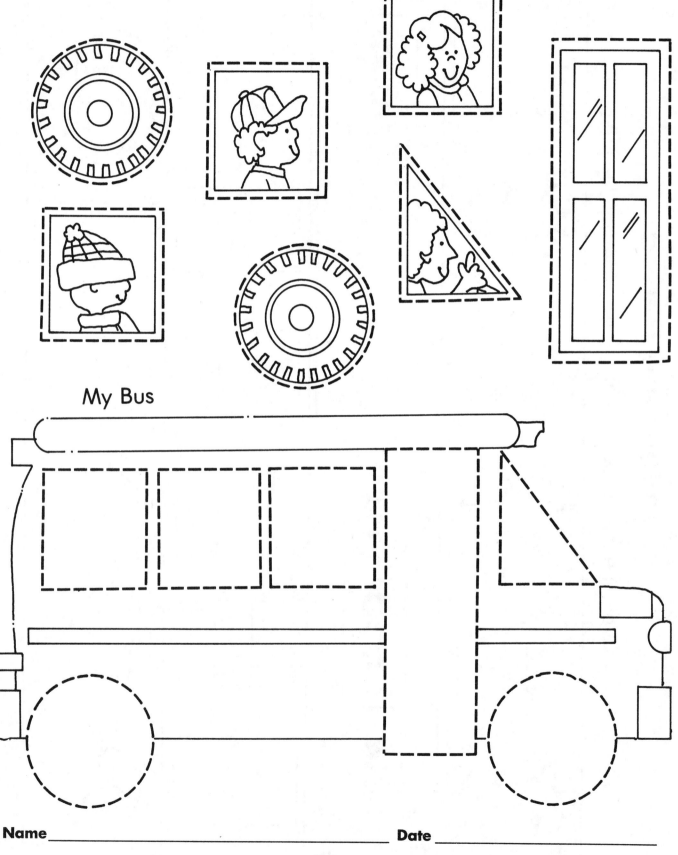

My Bus

Puppet Shapes

Find all the hidden circles, squares, triangles, and rectangles in this picture. Color the squares blue. Color the circles red. Color the triangles and rectangles yellow.

Cut the Shapes

Color these shapes. Then cut the shapes out and attach each where it belongs on the next page.

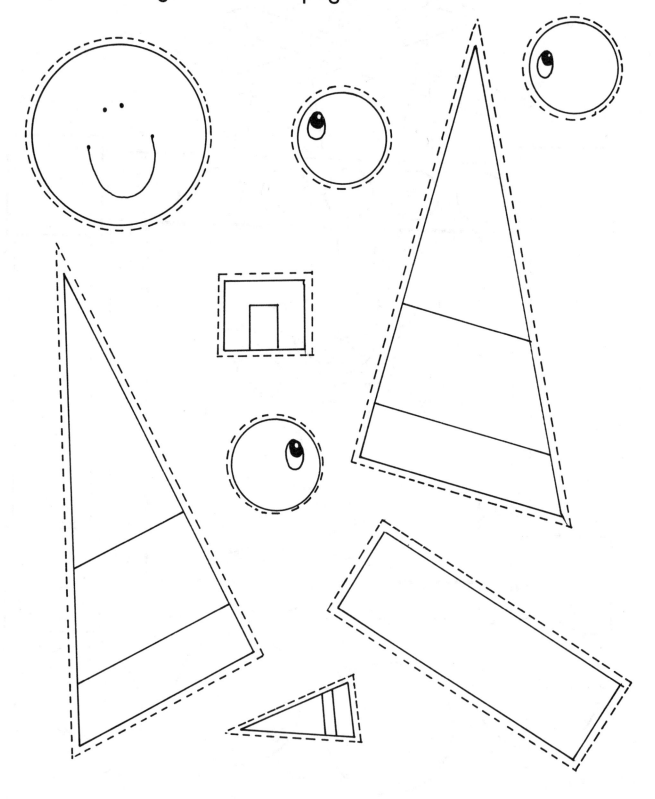

Name_____ **Date**_____

28

Copyright © 1995 by Troll Associates

Paste the Shapes

Attach all the squares (□), circles (○), triangles (△),
and rectangles (▭) where they fit in this picture.

Name_____ Date_____

29

All in a Row
Color what is different in each row.

Name_____ **Date**_____

What's Alike?

Color the two objects that look the same in each row.

Name_____ Date_____

33

Something's Different

Color the two objects that look the same in each row.

Name_____ **Date**_____

What's the Same?

Color the two objects that are the same in each row.

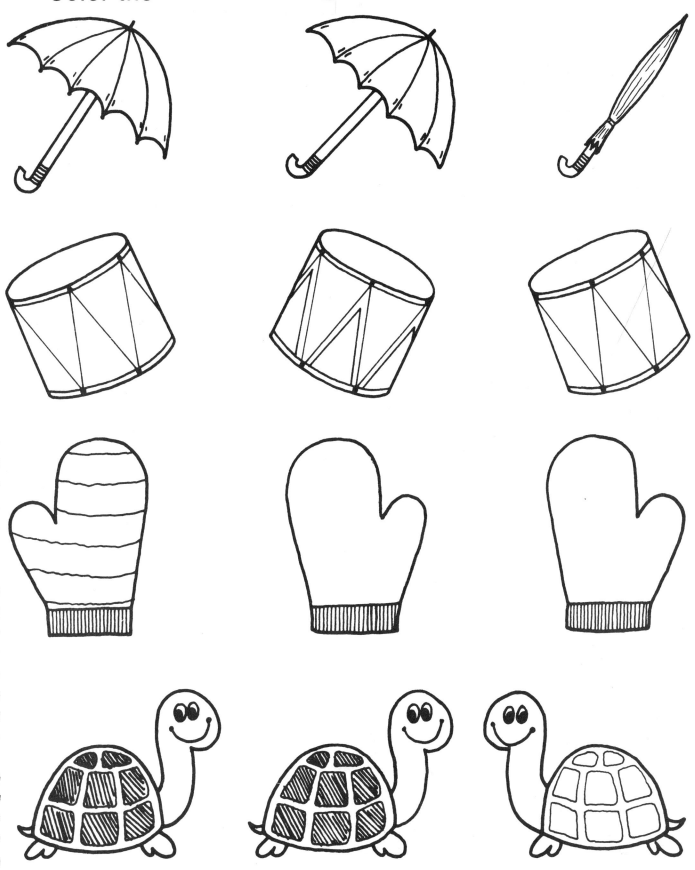

Name _____   Date _____

35

Big, Big, Bigger

Color what looks different in each row.

 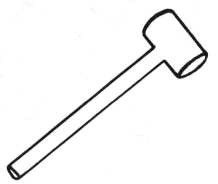 

Name_____ Date_____

Mystery Match

Color the two objects that look the same in each row.

Name_____ **Date** _____

Where Are the Twins?

Two shapes in each row are alike.
Color them.

Name_____ **Date** _____

Where Is the Stranger?

One shape in each row looks different. Color it.

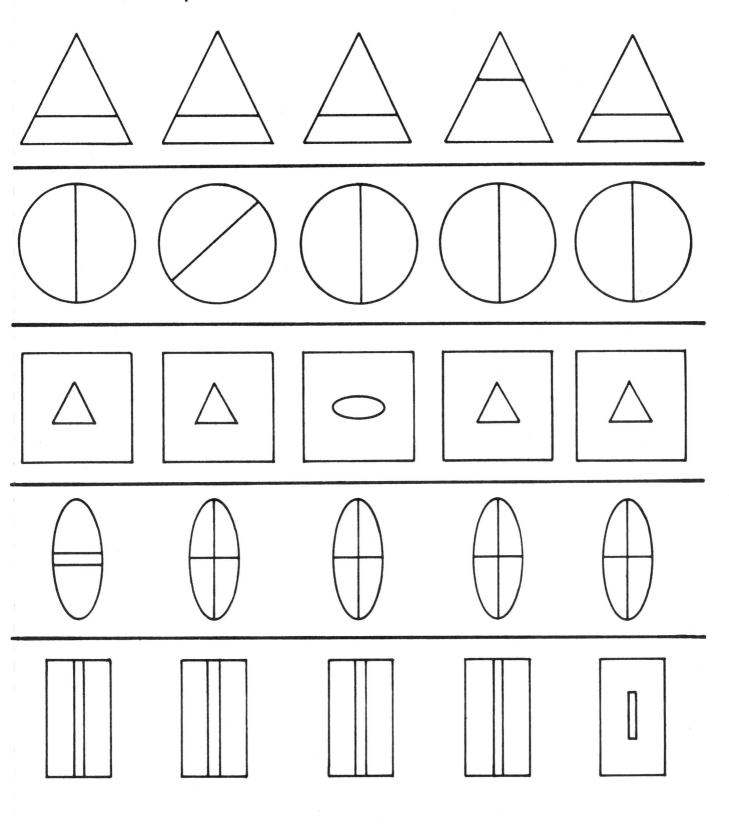

Name_____ Date _____

Two of the Same

Two shapes in each row are alike. Color them.

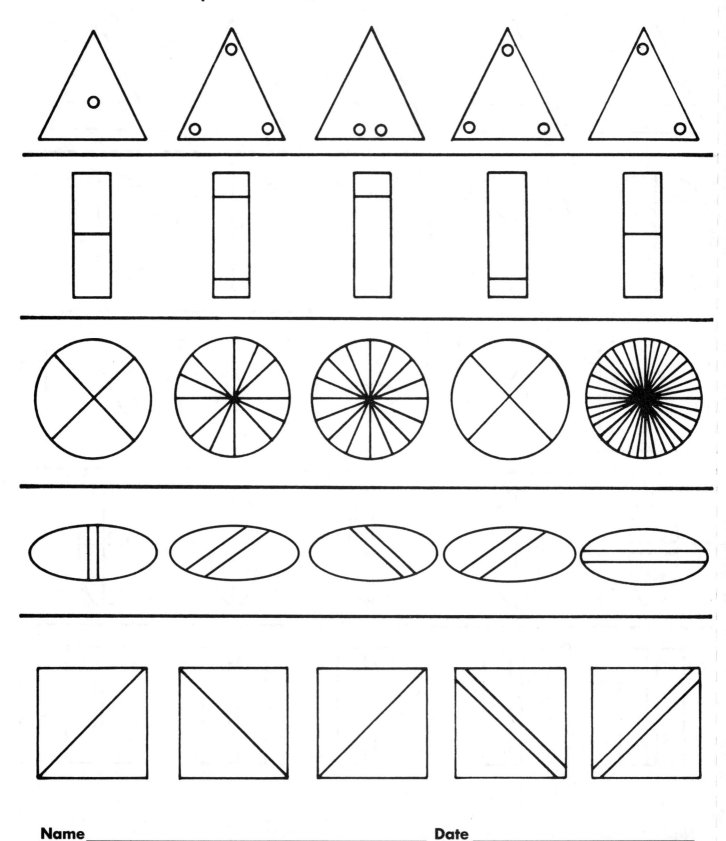

Name_____ **Date** _____

Someone's Hiding

One shape in each row looks different. Color it.

Name_____ **Date** _____

41

Alphabet Fun

APPLE

This letter is **A**. Write **A**.

Alphabet Fun

This letter is **B**. Write **B**.

BOOK

Alphabet Fun

CAT

This letter is C. Write C.

Name_____   Date _____

Alphabet Fun

This letter is **D**. Write **D**.

DOG

Name

Date

Alphabet Fun

This letter is E. Write E.

ELEPHANT

Name_____   Date _____

 # Alphabet Fun

FOX

This letter is F. Write F.

Name_____ Date _____

Alphabet Fun

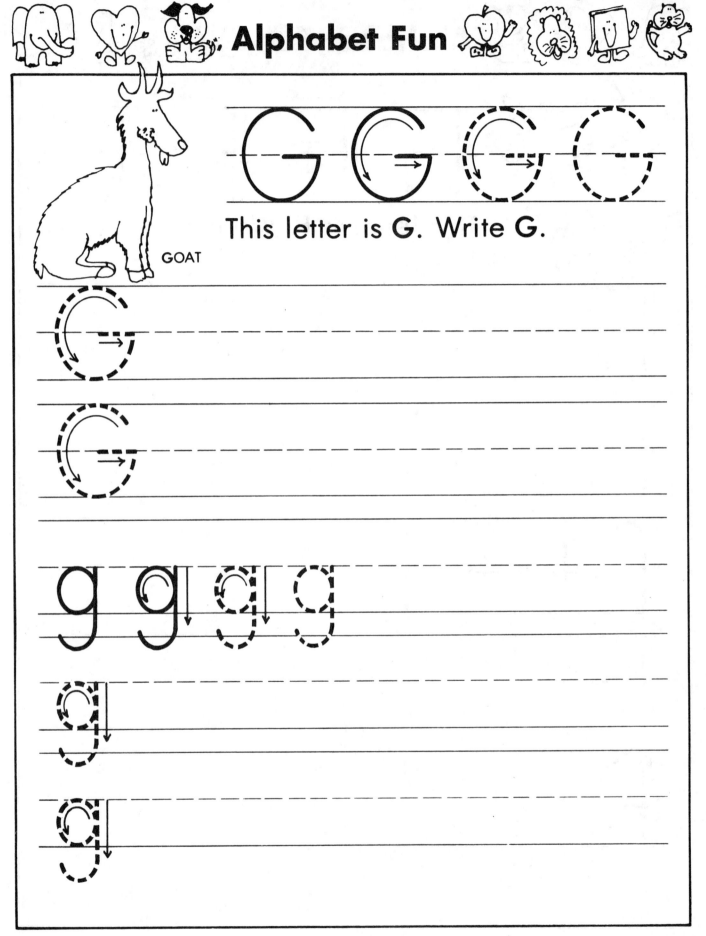

GOAT

This letter is **G**. Write **G**.

Name_____ Date _____

Alphabet Fun

This letter is H. Write H.

HEART

Name_____ Date _____

Alphabet Fun

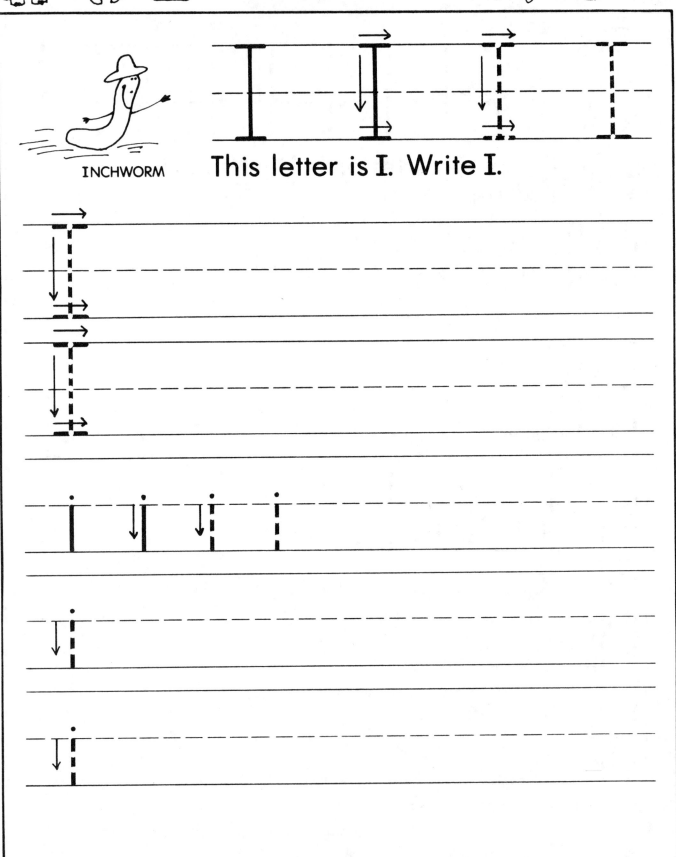

INCHWORM

This letter is I. Write I.

Name_____ Date _____

Alphabet Fun

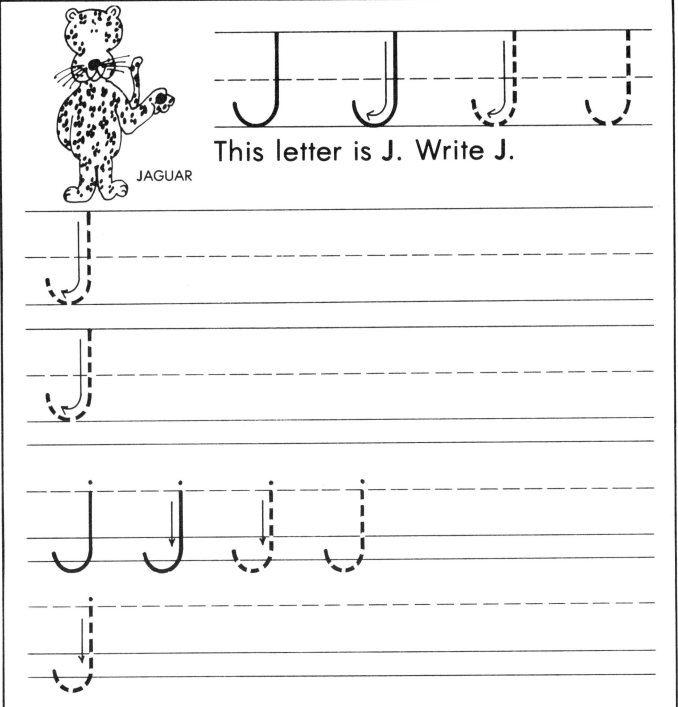

This letter is J. Write J.

JAGUAR

Name _____ Date _____

Alphabet Fun

This letter is K. Write K.

KANGAROO

Name_____   **Date**_____

Alphabet Fun

This letter is L. Write L.

LION

Alphabet Fun

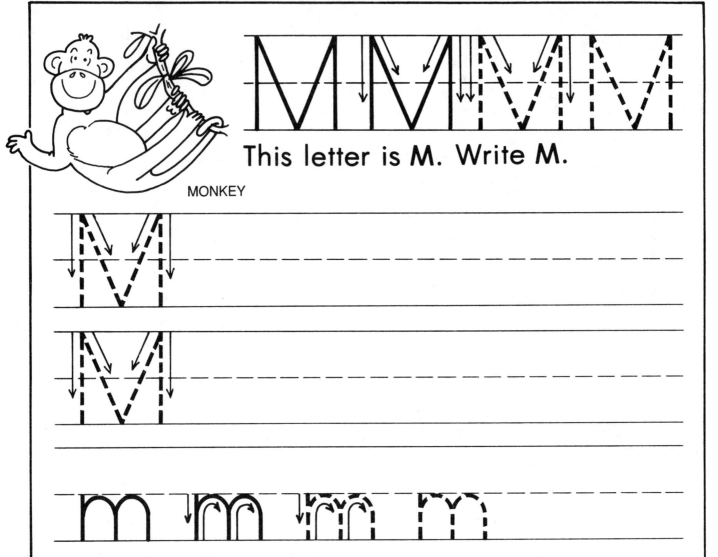

This letter is **M.** Write **M.**

MONKEY

Alphabet Fun

NEST

This letter is N. Write N.

Alphabet Fun

ONION

This letter is O. Write O.

Name_____ **Date** _____

Alphabet Fun

P P P P

This letter is P. Write P.

PENGUIN

P

P

p p p p

Name_____ **Date** _____

Alphabet Fun

QUAIL

This letter is Q. Write Q.

Name_____   Date _____

Alphabet Fun

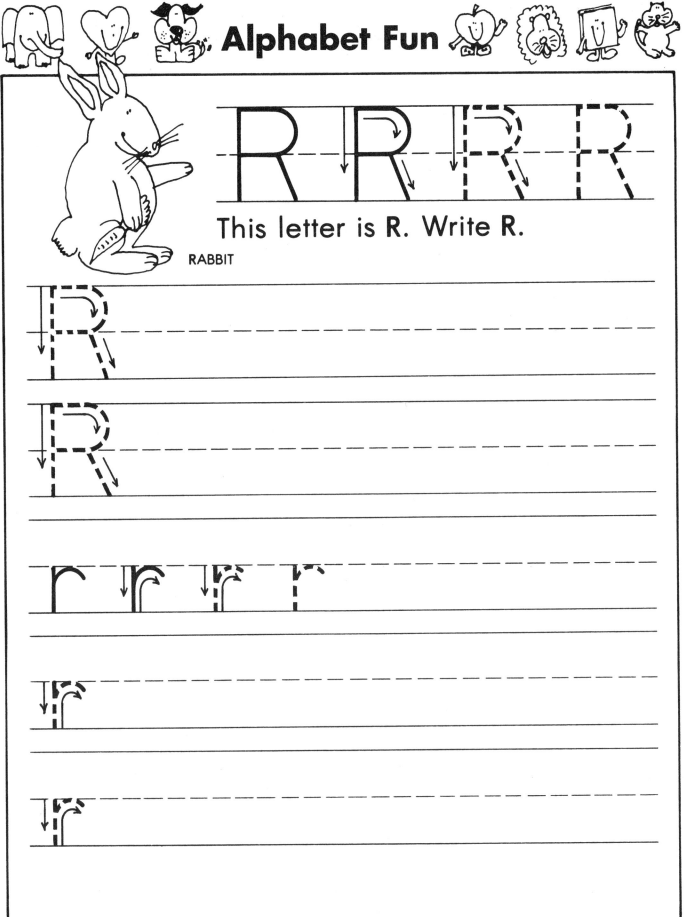

R R R R R

This letter is R. Write R.

RABBIT

Name _____ Date _____

Alphabet Fun

S S S S S

This letter is S. Write S.

SQUARE

S

S

S S S S

S

S

Name_____ Date_____

60

Alphabet Fun

This letter is T. Write T.

TIGER

Name_____ Date _____

Alphabet Fun

This letter is **U**. Write **U**.

UMBRELLA

Name_____ Date _____

Alphabet Fun

VULTURE

This letter is V. Write V.

Alphabet Fun

This letter is W. Write W.

WALRUS

Name _____ **Date** _____

Alphabet Fun

YO-YO

ZERO

XYLOPHONE

This is X. Write X.

This is Y. Write Y.

This is Z. Write Z.

Name _____ Date _____

 # Copy Cat

Copy each picture and each word.

house

snowman

pie

Name _____ **Date** _____

66

Make a Match

Two letters in each row are alike. Circle them.

P   K   U   T   P

* *

J   M   V   J   G

* *

S   R   S   U   K

* *

B   X   H   X   C

* *

O   T   N   T   Q

* *

A   F   I   V   F

Name_____ **Date**_____

Who Stands Out?

One letter in each row is different. Circle it.

M M M T M

* *

Q Q R Q Q

* *

B B B B K

* *

X T T T T

* *

L L M L L

* *

J I J J J

Name_____ Date _____

Letter Line-Up

Two letters in each row are alike. Circle them.

a   a   t   q   m

* *

e   o   p   r   e

* *

l   x   d   d   b

* *

c   r   m   n   m

* *

s   r   u   v   r

* *

d   b   k   d   l

Name_____ **Date** _____

One Stands Alone

One letter in each row is different. Circle it.

g   g   g   q   g

* *

i   j   i   i   i

* *

d   a   a   a   a

* *

h   h   n   h   h

* *

p   b   b   b   b

* *

r   n   r   r   r

Name_____ **Date** _____

70

Two's a Pair

Two words in each row are alike. Circle them.

fat   cat   bat   hat   bat

* *

hit   kit   sit   hit   fit

* *

see   me   tea   key   key

* *

say   may   way   may   ray

* *

met   pet   net   set   met

* *

sell   bell   tell   bell   fell

Name_____ **Date** _____

Find the Word

One word in each row is different. Circle it.

rice   rice   sun   rice   rice

* *

look   hook   hook   hook   hook

* *

to   to   to   if   to

* *

way   top   way   way   way

* *

fun   fun   fit   fun   fun

* *

small   tall   tall   tall   tall

Name_____ **Date** _____

Where Is That Word?

One word in each row is different. Circle it.

hot   hut   hot   hot   hot

****

rag   rag   ray   rag   rag

****

bag   bag   bag   bag   bug

****

car   can   car   car   car

****

truck   trick   truck   truck   truck

****

sun   son   son   son   son

Name_____ **Date** _____

Word Pals

Two words in each row are alike. Circle them.

then   then   them   they   the

* *

this   that   the   their   this

* *

what   when   where   what   who

* *

he   her   him   she   him

* *

we   us   our   they   us

* *

did   does   do   does   done

Name_____ Date _____

Letters on Parade

Two letters in each column are alike.
Circle them.

A	B	L	P	O
D	S	E	R	E
F	Z	Q	B	Q
G	M	O	R	O
E	N	F	D	C
F	Z	L	M	D

Hide & Seek

Two letters in each column are alike.
Circle them.

a	f	e	z	l
b	p	c	s	i
d	g	o	m	t
e	q	e	n	b
p	l	p	m	p
b	g	r	t	t

Name_____ **Date** _____

76